This is a must-read:  depression, a must-re you don't know, and or a friend. The author deals delicately about the complexity and longevity of depression, weaving it through the complexity of her own story and the complexity of the Psalms – helping us walk with our Saviour through the various valleys we encounter. Just read it - it's very real, very honest, very practical, very biblical, and very helpful.

Rev Innes Macsween
Assistant Minister, Smithton Church, Inverness

When mental health concerns are rife amongst teenagers, this is a timely little book. Rachel Lane shows a deep concern for young people struggling with depression, and is wonderfully honest as she draws from the experience of her own teenage years. The book is full of wise counsel, practical help, and gospel truth, while also being easy to read and accessible for all teens, regardless of Christian faith. I pray that this book will help teens battling with mental health issues to open up and speak to someone. Above all, I pray that it would steer them towards the gracious and loving care of God himself.

Rich Arnold, Youth and Families Minister,
Holy Cross Church, Hove

The statistics say that many (or most) of our young people will experience at least some symptoms of depression. In this book those young people will find the gentleness, warmth and understanding that only comes from hard experience. They will also find Christ and the promise that he can be their good shepherd through the darkest places. My prayer is that parents and young people hear the comfort and hope that this book points them to.

Ed Drew, Director of Faith in Kids
and formerly Children's Worker at Dundonald Church,
South West London

With so many teenagers suffering from mental health problems it feels very timely to read Rachel lane's book on her own story of teenage depression. Personal, engaging and beautifully honest it explores the reality of what depression looks and feels like. This book gives hope to those who might be suffering both through what professionals may offer with medical help and psychological support, but also the hope that the God of the bible can give us, the God who not only understands our struggles but who helps us within them.

Dr Tracey Foy, GP and minister's wife, East Sussex

Warm, accessible and wise, this is a great resource for young people facing depression and those who care for them. It's a little book but packed with Bible teaching, personal experience and practical advice.

Emma Scrivener, author of several books,
including *A New Name*, and *A New Day*, (IVP)

It is a most difficult and distressing experience to see a loved one overwhelmed by depression and feel unable to help. It is most helpful to have someone who understands, who has been there (more than once,) who can describe the territory and explain the experience, identifying things that can help and things that do not help; offering suggestions and encouragement. Seeing the need for God in all this yet being realistic and honest that being a Christian does not grant immunity from depression but does offer hope that even this can be used for good. I do believe that this book will be a real help for those struggling with depression either in themselves or in those they love. Although it specifically focuses on depression in adolescent years it contains much that is valuable in understanding and dealing with depression at any age.

Dr Andrew Risbridger,
psychiatrist working in community mental
health services in the UK

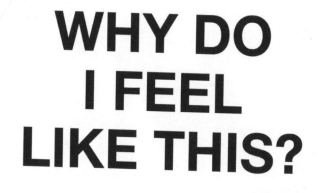

WHY DO I FEEL LIKE THIS?

WHY DO I FEEL LIKE THIS?

Meeting God in the emptiness

RACHEL LANE

CHRISTIAN
FOCUS

10 9 8 7 6 5 4 3 2 1

Copyright © 2020 Rachel Lane
Paperback ISBN: 978-1-5271-0617-8
Epub ISBN: 978-1-5271-0667-3
Mobi ISBN: 978-1-0668-0

Published by Christian Focus Publications,
Geanies House, Fearn, Tain, Ross-shire,
IV20 1TW, Scotland, U.K.
www.christianfocus.com;
email: info@christianfocus.com

Cover design by Pete Barnsley
Cover photo by Sergio Santana on Unsplash

Printed and bound by
Bell and Bain, Glasgow

Contents

For Mum and Dad. You walked a hard road alongside me, with courage and unwavering love. I'm more grateful than I can ever say.

INTRODUCTION

I've thought about writing this book for a long time.

I've always loved to write. When I was a little girl, it was stories. Later on, I kept a journal. But by the time I reached my twenties, I felt like I had no words left. I wanted to write again, but I didn't know what I wanted to say.

'Write about what you know,' is the advice often given to aspiring authors. The idea held little appeal.

'I know about depression,' I thought. 'I know about messing things up. I know about hurting. I know about hurting other people. I know about wasted opportunities. I know about regrets.'

It was hard to believe that anyone would want to read that book. Even if they did, I wasn't ready to write it.

So why now?

Mainly, it's because I keep hearing about young boys and girls a bit like I was. Young people who are struggling with depression and other mental health issues. And their parents who are desperate to help but don't know how.

I am now a mother myself, and before long my own children will be teenagers. It seems that the kind of problems I struggled with have only become more common in the intervening years. The world is changing fast, and new technologies have brought new challenges for young people. I don't have all the answers, and I can't pretend that I do. But I want to share what I do have.

Because, by God's grace, I know about depression, but I also know about things getting better. I know about hurting people, but I also know about restored relationships. I know about wasted opportunities, but I also know about new ones.

If you or someone that you care about are suffering from depression, my prayer is that this book might give you hope.

I don't know what you believe about God. Maybe you would call yourself a Christian, or maybe you wouldn't. Maybe you have grown up in a Christian family, but aren't sure yet what you make of it all. That's okay. There will hopefully be things in this book that you might relate to, and that might help you, regardless of what you believe.

At the same time, there will also be stuff about God, and the Bible. Even if you're not too sure what you think about that, I'd encourage you to give those parts of the book a chance. You might find that God understands your depression better than you realise. You might even find, as I did eventually, that he is the best source of help there is.

I waited patiently for the Lord;
he turned to me and heard my cry.
He lifted me out of the slimy pit,
out of the mud and mire;
he set my feet on a rock
and gave me a firm place to stand.
He put a new song in my mouth,
a hymn of praise to our God.
Many will see and fear the Lord
and put their trust in him
(Psalm 40:1-3).

WHAT'S HAPPENING TO ME?

I didn't want to get out of bed.

I felt like I couldn't get out of bed. I couldn't face school. I could barely face leaving my bedroom. Instead, I lay on my bed for hours on end, listening to the same two sad songs on my stereo. Sometimes, I sat in front of the mirror and watched myself cry, with a mixture of self-pity and fascination. Other times, I couldn't even cry. I just felt numb, empty. Or plain terrified.

I think my parents were pretty terrified too. They were certainly bewildered. What had happened to their happy little girl? The little girl they nicknamed 'Rae Beam' because of her sunny smile and chirpy disposition?

One day, a day when I should have been at school but had refused to go, my godmother came to visit. She lived a long way away and I didn't know her very well. I wasn't up to seeing anyone, but I remember being a bit surprised that I wasn't even asked to come downstairs. Later, when I asked about it, I was told that she hadn't come to see me, but to see my mum. To talk and pray with her ... *about* me. I think that's when I realised how worried my parents must be. I was their third child, but this was new territory. They simply didn't know what to do.

That was the summer I turned thirteen. I can't remember exactly when it began, or when it ended, but it did end. I started back at school in September and I was 'okay'. No one had used the word 'depression', not then. It wasn't until something similar happened again, around two years later, and then again, a couple of years after that, that I began to associate what was happening with that word.

What is depression?

'Depression' can be a confusing term, because people have come to use it to mean two quite different things. We often say that we feel 'depressed' and just mean that we feel sad, or down. Everyone feels like that from time to time, but usually it doesn't last for long; maybe a few hours, or a few days at the most. That can lead to a lot of misunderstanding when people are diagnosed with what is sometimes called 'clinical depression'. It might sound as though that person is just in a particularly long and exaggerated low mood. Which is sort of true. And yet most people who have struggled with depression would agree that this description doesn't really cover it.

So how do we describe what 'depression' is like? The thing is, everyone who suffers from it has their own unique experience. There will be common ground, but there can also be a lot that is different from person to person. That makes it even more difficult to explain or define.

Many people have tried, and you might find some of their descriptions helpful.

'It's like falling down a well with no bottom; the blackness surrounds you and the tiny circle of light gets ever smaller until it disappears.'

'It's like dragging round a massive stone, holding you back and weighing you down. Like when you're at the gym and you just can't see how you can push forward with even one more rep, and everyone else around you is doing fine.'

'It is like someone came along and stole all the pleasure in my life. The things I used to enjoy become empty and meaningless and it is a struggle just to exist. Every ounce of strength goes on just getting to the end of the day and I feel like a battery that never gets enough time to fully recharge before I am using the energy again.'

'It feels like you're drowning but no one can see, and the ones that can see shout "just swim!"'

'It can be like having the top layer of my skin removed. Everything feels much more sensitive: for me it's like everything people say points to me being disgusting or worthless.'[1]

These descriptions of depression by sufferers were posted recently on a popular website. But depression is nothing new. Charles Spurgeon, a well-known Christian preacher in the nineteenth century, often wrote about the low periods he went through. 'I could weep by the hour like a child, and yet I knew not what I wept for,'[2] he wrote. Elsewhere he says, 'The iron bolt ... mysteriously fastens the door of hope and holds our spirits in gloomy prison.'[3]

The writer William Styron famously described his depression as 'a veritable howling tempest

1. Blurt Team, 'Describing Depression to those who've never had it', The Blurt Foundation, 2016, https://www.blurtitout.org/2016/07/08/describing-depression-whove-never/ (accessed 20 March 2020).
2. Quoted in Edward T. Welch, *Depression: A Stubborn Darkness* (New Growth Press, 2004), p. 21.
3. C.H. Spurgeon, *Lectures to My Students* (Christian Focus Publications, Tain, 2018), p.187.

in the brain'[4]. Pastor and author Mark Meynell calls it 'a brain blizzard.'[5] Elsewhere he uses the metaphor of a volcano, because depression 'may lie relatively dormant for some time' but then 'without warning ... I'll be caught out by an eruption of psychological pain. It feels like sudden grief and despair without an immediately obvious loss. Or it might manifest as uncontrollable anxiety and dread.'[6]

Yet at other times, depression can feel like a complete lack of emotion. 'It can be quieter for some people,' writes counsellor Ed Welch. 'Instead of a bottomless abyss and howling in the brain, life is flat, gray and cold. Nothing holds any interest. You are a barely walking zombie. Everything is drab, lifeless and tired. Why work? Why get out of bed? Why do anything? Nothing seems to matter.'[7]

---

4. William Styron, *Darkness Visible: A Memoir of Madness* (Vintage Classics, 2001 edn), p. 37.
5. Mark Meynell, When Darkness Seems My Closest Friend (IVP, 2008), p. 25.
6. Ibid, p. 26.
7. Edward T. Welch, Depression (NGP, 2004), p. 24-25.

The author Elizabeth Wurtzel described it in a similar way. 'Depression ... involves a complete absence: absence of affect, absence of feeling, absence of response, absence of interest.'[8]

What about you?

Perhaps as you read these descriptions of depression, they seem a bit 'over the top'. Or perhaps some of them ring true, and you've experienced feeling this way yourself. Or maybe you know other people who talk about feeling like this.

It might be helpful to think of 'depression' as being on a spectrum or scale ranging from mild to moderate and then to severe.

In that case, some of the descriptions above would represent the moderate to severe end of the spectrum. Many people suffer from mild depression from time to time, and they may find they can manage

8. Elizabeth Wurtzel, Prozac Nation: Young & Depressed in America (Quartet Books, 1996), p. 14.

it with some self-help strategies and lifestyle changes, which we'll talk more about later. But if depression persists and gets worse, it may have slipped into more moderate or severe depression. At this stage, it is often harder for the sufferer to help themselves. They might struggle to think clearly enough to make sensible decisions about the way ahead. They need help.

It is important to say here that severe depression can make it impossible to function normally. It is a very strange and frightening place to be. It can be every bit as incapacitating as a broken leg or any other 'visible' health problem. Not only does the sufferer have to contend with their own mental anguish, but they often meet with a lack of understanding, because their problem can't be seen and is so hard to explain or describe.

If you think you might be depressed, wherever you may fall on the spectrum, I would encourage you to talk to somebody. Preferably a parent or another understanding adult. Tell them how you feel. I would also strongly encourage you to see your doctor. That might feel like an awkward or embarrassing prospect, but try to push those feelings to one side. Your doctor will be very used to speaking with young people who are struggling with symptoms of anxiety and depression. According to a UK database for doctors, depressive feelings are very common in adolescence, with up to half of 14 to 15-year-olds feeling miserable, a quarter self-critical and 8% experiencing suicidal thoughts.[9]

If you find it difficult to talk to your particular doctor, consider trying to find a different one. When I was sixteen, I moved to a different surgery so that I could see a doctor who had been recommended to us. It was definitely worth it.

Seeking help is not about being weak – it's about being wise. It's estimated that only about 15% of depressed people get treatment, but

---

9. General Practice Notebook, 'Childhood Depression (Epidemiology)', Oxford Solutions Ltd, 2016 https://gpnotebook.com/simplepage. cfm?ID=1798635525&linkID=11883&cook=yes (accessed 26 March 2020).

of those people, at least 70% get better[10]. And remember that treatment doesn't necessarily involve taking medication. We'll talk more about types of treatment in the chapter 'What helps?', but it's important to know that taking antidepressant medication is just one of the options, to be considered under the advice and supervision of your doctor.

Symptoms of depression

We've already seen that depression looks different for different people. But there are several symptoms that are common to many. If you do go and visit your doctor, they will probably ask you about some of these. They might also ask you to fill in a short questionnaire to help them understand what you've been going through.

- Persistent low mood – feeling sad or angry most of the time.

- No longer enjoying things that you used to enjoy.

---

10. Nicola Morgan, *Blame My Brain: The Amazing Teenage Brain Revealed* (Walker Books, 2013 edition), p.151.

- Sleep problems – especially struggling to get to sleep or waking up early, and being unable to get back to sleep.

- Feeling tired all the time.

- Appetite changes – not feeling hungry, or overeating (sometimes referred to as 'comfort eating').

- Isolating yourself from social situations and not wanting to go out.

- Struggling to concentrate or think clearly.

- Feelings of guilt or unworthiness.

- Feeling like hurting yourself, or actually hurting yourself.

- Thinking about death, or considering different ways of taking your own life.

You may have experienced several of these, or only one or two. If either of the last two statements apply to you, **PLEASE** seek help straight away. Speak to a parent if possible, but if not then a teacher, doctor, or any other responsible adult. At the back of this book there are the phone numbers of several helplines. You can call them and speak to someone anonymously. Whatever you do, please seek help. You will not always feel this way. There is life on the other side of this, and it's worth living.

Do I have 'depression'?

Reading through this chapter might have helped you to think about whether you could be suffering from depression, but it's important to get a proper diagnosis from a doctor. It's normal to experience emotional 'ups and downs' ... in fact you wouldn't be human if you didn't! These ups and downs can seem particularly exaggerated during adolescence, and we're going to look more at that in the next chapter. But feeling low is common and doesn't necessarily mean that you have depression.

If you have been diagnosed with depression, try not to let the 'label' bother you. It could be a positive thing if it means that you can get the help you need, but it doesn't define you. This is not 'who you are'.

Remember the spectrum we looked at. People move up and down that spectrum over the course of their lives. Some might never experience being at the 'severe' end, but many, many people will. For some, it's through a broken relationship or losing someone they love. For some it's through abuse, or physical illness. For others, it may be through clinical depression or anxiety.

Whatever the cause of your emotional pain, you are not alone.

Songs for the Brokenhearted

At the beginning of this chapter, I admitted that I used to listen to certain sad songs, over and over again. Looking back it seems obvious that perhaps this wasn't the most constructive idea, but the music seemed to express something of what I was feeling inside.

I wish that someone had pointed me instead to the songbook of the Bible, the Book of Psalms. These songs, composed more than two thousand years ago, are still a source of great help to people today. There are many songs of praise, thankfulness and rejoicing.

But plenty of the Psalms also express negative emotions, emotions that are described in raw and powerful ways:

> I am worn out from my groaning.
> All night long I flood my bed with weeping
> and drench my couch with tears.
> My eyes grow weak with sorrow;
> they fail because of all my foes
> (Psalm 6:6).

> My tears have been my food day and night,
> while people say to me all day long,
> 'Where is your God?'
> (Psalm 42:3)

> I sink in the miry depths,
> where there is no foothold.
> I have come into the deep waters;
> the floods engulf me
> (Psalm 69:2).

Some of these words don't sound so different to the descriptions of depression we looked at earlier, do they? They are the words of people in pain; not only physical pain, but mental anguish too. As well as describing their suffering, the writers of the Psalms ask questions, even questions of God, that many people would be afraid to ask:

Why, Lord, do you stand far off?
Why do you hide yourself in times of trouble?
(Psalm 10:1).

How long, Lord? Will you forget me for ever?
How long will you hide your face from me?
How long must I wrestle with my thoughts
and day after day have sorrow in my heart?
(Psalm 13:1)

Now it's obvious when we read the Psalms that David and the other men who wrote them were going through some pretty tough things. David – the same David who fought the giant Goliath, later to be King David – had a lot of enemies. Some of these songs were written while he was on the run, or in hiding, in fear of his very life.

The trials we are facing may seem quite different, but that doesn't mean the Psalms aren't relevant to us. Everything that is in the Bible has been included for a reason, and the amazing thing is that God can speak to us through it directly today, no matter who we are or what circumstances we face. The fact that this book of songs is in the Bible tells us that God does not disapprove of strong emotions. He made every part of us, including our capacity to feel things deeply. But he wants to show us, through the psalmists, what to do with those emotions. Ultimately, he wants to teach us to bring them to him.

Something to try...

I know that it can be hard to read the Bible or pray when you're struggling with depression. It can be hard to concentrate on anything. If that is a particular battle for you at the moment, I would still encourage you to try just doing the first of these suggestions.

Ask a friend or family member if they would read a Psalm aloud to you. If you aren't sure which to choose, try starting with Psalm 23, Psalm 27 or Psalm 121.

If you are able, read some of the Psalms yourself. In this chapter I have only dipped into a very few; there are 150 altogether! You could start with the ones suggested, or look for others that speak to you personally.

At the end of each chapter of this book, there will be suggestions of things that you could do to put some of the ideas into practice. These are completely optional, and if you have severe depression at the moment they may well feel like too much. You can simply ignore them or return to them at a later date.

Something to remember...

We can be honest with God. He knows how we feel, and he wants us to cry out to him in our pain.

What did Jesus say?

Ask and it will be given to you; seek and you will find; knock and the door will be opened to you (Matthew 7:7).

WHY NOW?

If there was one subject Rachel struggled with at school it was Maths.

This was a joke my dad would dish out on a regular basis. 'Never better demonstrated than when she started her teenage rebellion at eleven, rather than thirteen!'

Well, I don't know about that, but I certainly began to change a lot around that age. Then again, things around me had changed a lot too. For a start I faced the enormous transition most eleven-year-olds in the UK undergo, from primary to secondary school. I'd looked forward to going, especially as my best friend Jane from down the road would finally be at the same school. We'd practised the cycle ride together throughout the summer before, and were all ready with our matching helmets, shiny shoes, and backpacks nearly as big as we were! But as it happened, Jane was placed in the other half of the year to me. There were nine forms, and we didn't have a single class together. I was on my own.

Still, I made other friends, in time. I started being allowed to go places with them, swimming or into town, *without my parents*. I stayed over at their houses. I started listening to different music, swapping the cheesy pop tunes I'd once enjoyed for darker, moodier songs. I put posters of men I liked on my bedroom walls, black and white shots of actors leaning against their motorbikes. My body was changing too, and fast. I was beginning to look more like a woman, even if I still felt like a little girl inside. I experimented with different kinds of clothes, imitating the older girls I admired who swept past me arm-in-arm in the corridors, or leaned against the bicycle sheds chatting to their boyfriends.

My efforts to be cool must have paid off. A popular (if not particularly attractive) boy in my year had a crush on me. I was flattered, but anxious. He followed me home one day with his friends, but I hid upstairs and wouldn't come to the door. Somehow they found out my phone number and I got a call from a girl I didn't know. 'He's really nice you know,' she assured me. 'I went out with him at primary school.' But I wasn't interested, and just wanted the whole thing to go away.

Not long after that I dyed my hair for the first time, with henna. It turned a lovely copper colour, but smelt of plants when it got wet. Still, I liked it. Plus, it had the unexpected side effect of repelling my not-so-secret admirer. He decided to stop asking me out and start calling me 'Baked Bean Head' instead, a nickname which, sadly, would follow me throughout my secondary school years.

Everything's changing

The years of life often described as young adulthood or adolescence are a time of rapid change on a number of levels. Our bodies are changing, growing and developing in ways that we may or may not appreciate. (New curves? Muscles? Yes please. Acne? Not so much!). Our brains are changing, flooding our bodies with the hormones we need for reproduction later on. We no longer feel like children but are not yet treated as adults. We may crave more independence from our parents. We may long for excitement and even risk, or wish we were credited with more responsibility. We may start questioning things we took for granted during our younger years. We might start wondering who we really are, and thinking about who we *want* to be.

I have used the words 'may' and 'might' because most of these statements are generalisations. Everyone is different. Some people seem to sail through their teenage years, while others find themselves on an emotional roller-coaster they don't remember buying a ticket for ... and don't seem to be able to get off! But however the changes affect us, there's no mistaking the fact that during this stage of life, we *are* changing.

Scientists are finding out new things all the time about what is going on in our bodies during this unique period of development. Even if you aren't that keen on science (it was never my strong point), it's really helpful to learn a bit more about these physical changes and how they might impact our emotions. We can't reduce everything to biology, but it does have its part to play.

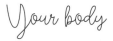

Your body

The changes that happen to our bodies as we mature into adults can be very unpredictable. Puberty usually hits girls earlier than boys, sometimes starting as early as 8 years old, although it can be much later. Boys can also start anywhere between the ages of 9 and 14, with changes in the genital area usually being the first sign of puberty. Female growth spurts also happen earlier, so girls may enjoy a year or two of towering over the boys before it all changes again! Some of the things that are happening to our bodies may be easier to keep to ourselves, while others are only too conspicuous. It's natural to feel self-conscious when our figure is obviously changing shape, or we're battling with spots, or our voice is breaking and we don't know when what we have to say might come out as a squeak or a croak (granted, I never experienced that one myself, but it sounds tricky!). And all this is playing out in front of our peer group, day in, day out. The only consolation is that most of them will be going through the same things themselves!

I felt like my body changed very fast. I had always been small for my age, so it was something of a relief to suddenly shoot up to the height of an average grown woman between the ages of about 12 and 14. As for the changes to my body shape ... well, like many young girls I had mixed feelings about those. It made me feel grown up, and I liked the idea that the opposite sex might be attracted to me. But my best friend at the time was very skinny, and so was her older sister whom I secretly idolised. There was no social media to feed my obsession with body image, but TV, films and magazines did enough. It was the era of the 'waif', when a new wave of supermodels presented an ideal of female beauty to which most of us could never aspire. So I started every day on a diet, from the age of about 12. My chosen method of self-starvation was pretty hard on my growing body, so for several years those diets didn't get very far. In fact, they usually ended with a Mars bar and a bag of marshmallows on the way home from school.

Acne was another trial. I was fortunate not to get many spots until my later teens, but then my skin more than made up for lost time. The spots I tended to get were what are called acne cysts – huge, red lumps that could be felt ominously throbbing under the skin long before anything made it to the surface. Impossible to hide, though I tried hard. Impossible to forget, when they were often painful as well. The effect they had on my self-esteem was disastrous. Maybe I shouldn't have cared so much, but I did. It was years before I discovered treatments that actually worked, having paid many a visit to the GP and dermatologist. If this is a struggle for you, and it is making you miserable, I would encourage you to see your doctor too. A lot of people think that having acne is just 'one of those things', but moderate to severe acne can have a significant impact on the mental health of those who suffer from it. Although there is no cure, there are treatments that can help a great deal.

Your brain

We all know that hormones can have a huge effect on our emotions, and are often blamed for the mood swings many suffer from in their teens. But other changes most of us know less about are also taking place within the teenage brain. Scientists have found that during this stage of life, the most dramatic changes seem to be taking place in the *prefrontal cortex*, the part of the brain that is most associated with *thinking, reasoning, logic* and *decision-making*.

Firstly, there is a huge amount of growth in this area, an increase in what is called 'grey matter'. In fact, there seems to be so much growth that at a certain age, around 11-12, we end up with a lot more connections or synapses in our brain than we ultimately need. So over the next few years, a process of cutting back or 'pruning' occurs. If you are interested in reading about these changes in more detail, I'd strongly recommend Nicola Morgan's book *'Blame My Brain: The Amazing Teenage Brain Revealed'*[1]. She shows how these changes in the brain, particularly in the prefrontal cortex, may well be linked to various emotions and behaviours that seem to be more common in the teenage years.

For our purposes, it is sufficient to know that very significant changes in the brain are taking place at this stage of life.

Is that why I'm depressed?

As Nicola Morgan acknowledges, scientists are cautious about *assuming* connections

1. Nicola Morgan, *Blame My Brain: The Amazing Teenage Brain Revealed* (Walker Books, 2005).

between these brain changes and our emotions or behaviour. That doesn't mean they aren't connected. It's certainly true that when you have depression, you will often struggle to think clearly and rationally. It can feel difficult, even impossible, to make decisions. But as Morgan also points out, the rates of depression among adults are similar to those of teenagers – even though adults have a fully developed prefrontal cortex. If you have depression, the changes going on in your brain probably don't help, and may well affect how you express it. But that doesn't necessarily mean they are the *cause* of your depression.

What else is going on?

Our circumstances, the situations we are in and the things that are going on in our lives, also have a huge impact on how we feel. As well as being a time of great physical change, a lot of other things will be going during our teenage years.

I talked at the beginning of this chapter about changing schools, an experience that will be common to many. Like the majority of children in the UK, I went to a primary school where I had one teacher all the time, and was in the same class with pretty much the same thirty faces throughout. My secondary school was more than four times the size. I had a different teacher for every lesson, different classmates, and often a long way to walk in the five-minute changeover between periods (bowed down under my enormous backpack!). The only daily constant was my form tutor, the one with responsibility for my personal wellbeing. Unfortunately, if this lady had a nurturing bone in her body, I saw no evidence of it in the five years of our acquaintance. Each morning she swept in at the last moment of 'form time', perched on the edge of the desk with a sigh and took the register as quickly as possible, before sweeping out again. I had the distinct feeling that no one at school cared a jot about me.

On the other hand, I had a lot in my favour, even if I didn't always appreciate it at the time. My family life was stable, and - by and large - happy. My parents were together, happily married, and while we had no extended family close by, we were brought up going to church where we knew there were other adults who cared about us. We lived in a large house in a nice area and, after one significant move when I was five, we stayed put. My dad's job was secure and we always had enough money. My mum, a former teacher, stayed at home and poured almost all her time and energy into caring for the four of us children.

It wasn't long before I realised how different life was for many of my friends. One had lost her father at the age of six. Many had parents who were divorced. One had been abused by her stepfather, and arrived at our school when she had to move in with her dad. On top of family break ups, many of us face moves, health problems, friendship issues, bullying, or other challenges. All of these will affect the way we feel. As young adults, some of the biggest changes in our lives are things that we have little or no control over. Some of these may not be negative, but they still shape who we are and how we feel.

Of course, everyone reacts to things differently, and we'll talk more about that in the next chapter. Two people can go through a similar experience and both respond in very different ways. In some cases, our circumstances may trigger our depression, but they aren't the whole story either.

God and your circumstances

Your circumstances may not be the only factor in how you feel, but they do matter. The Bible teaches us that God knows all about the things we are going through, and that he cares.

In Psalm 31:9-13, David describes the difficult circumstances he finds himself in, and the effect they are having on him:

Be merciful to me, Lord, for I am in distress;
my eyes grow weak with sorrow,
my soul and body with grief.
My life is consumed by anguish
and my years by groaning;
my strength fails because of my affliction,
and my bones grow weak.
Because of all my enemies,
I am the utter contempt of my neighbours
and an object of dread to my closest friends –
those who see me on the street flee from me.
I am forgotten as though I were dead;
I have become like broken pottery.
For I hear many whispering,
'Terror on every side!'
They conspire against me
and plot to take my life.

There is no doubt here that David is 'up against it'. Whatever the particulars of his situation, we know that he finds himself alone, abandoned even by his closest friends and neighbours. Meanwhile he is facing formidable enemies, enemies who wish him dead!

But in the following verses, we see what he does with his fear and anguish. His next words are a prayer (Psalm 31:14-15):

But I trust in you, Lᴏʀᴅ;
I say, 'You are my God.'
My times are in your hands;
deliver me from the hands of my enemies,
from those who pursue me.

My times are in your hands.' David believed in a God who was in control, even of his most challenging circumstances. He knew that nothing that was happening to him was a surprise to God. That can be hard to get our heads round. If we are going through a difficult time, we often question where God is in it. Is there really a loving God? If so, why would he let us go through this? Why would he let this happen?

There are no easy answers to these questions. But notice that David doesn't turn away from God. He calls him *'my* God'. He trusts that God is listening to his prayer. He trusts that God can change things, that God can intervene in his situation. Only a God who is in control is a God who has the power to help us.

The God who helped David can help you too.

Something to try...

- Take some time to think about the things that are going on in your life at the moment. It might help, if you can, to write something down. Think about other significant events in your life that have had an impact on you. Do you think any of these things are contributing to how you feel now?

- If you can, consider talking to God about some of those things. It doesn't have to be a fancy prayer – God doesn't need us to use special words. Just talk to him as you would to anyone. If you have questions or doubts, that's okay. Like the writers of the Psalms, bring those questions to God.

- If you have a Christian parent, or friend, or church leader, consider asking them to pray with you and for you. It's up to you how much you share, of course, but if you can open up about some of the struggles you face it will probably help them to support you better.

Something to remember...

God knows everything that you are going through at the moment, and he cares. He wants to walk through this with you.

Our times are in Thy hand;
O God, we wish them there;
Our lives, our souls, our all, we leave
Entirely to Thy care.

Our times are in Thy hand:
Whatever they may be;
Pleasing or painful, dark or bright,
As best may seem to Thee.

Our times are in Thy hand;
Why should we doubt or fear?
A father's hand will never cause
His child a needless tear.

Our times are in Thy hand;
Jesus, the Crucified,
Whose hand our many sins have pierced,
Is now our guard and guide.

Our times are in Thy hand;
We'll always trust to Thee,
Till we possess the promised crown,
And all Thy glory see.

William Freeman Lloyd (1791-1853)

WHY ME?

I went through my most severe period of depression when I was sixteen.

I had just started studying for my A-levels. As things got worse and I had to drop one subject, then another, I felt like I was gradually dropping out of everything. Out of school, and out of life.

My two closest friends at that time responded very differently to what was going on. Katie understood – if not completely, enough to stick around. She'd been through some pretty tough times and was prone to depression herself. But Anna[1] was different. Instinctively, I didn't want to talk to her about how I was feeling; I

---

1. Name has been changed.

knew she wouldn't understand. We drifted apart, and later she admitted to a mutual friend that she just 'didn't get it'. I felt her disappointment, even anger; I wasn't the person she'd thought I was.

Anna had lost her father at a young age, her mum worked full time, and she and her brother had learnt to be very independent. She was 'tough as old boots' – opinionated, confident, and strong.

It felt as though there was an accusing finger pointing at me. What right did *I* – of all people – have to be depressed? I had a loving family, a comfortable home, bright prospects. Nothing particularly awful or tragic had ever happened to me. What on earth did I have to be depressed about?

I didn't blame her for not understanding. To be honest, I shared her confusion. What *was* wrong with me? Why couldn't I just 'get on with it' like everyone else?

We are all different

It's hard to understand why some people suffer from depression and others don't.

It's hard for those who struggle with depression, and wonder what is wrong with them. They compare themselves with others who seem to be coping and then feel weak and inadequate.

And it's also hard for those around them who *don't* tend to get depressed. Depression can seem like just self-pity or laziness. Many people would admit that at times they've found it difficult to understand why their depressed friend or family member can't just 'snap out of it' or 'pull themselves together'.

We've seen already that there are a variety of factors that can lead to depression. We might get depressed because of difficult things that happen to us, or because we're struggling with the symptoms of a physical illness, for instance. But it is also true that some people seem to be more prone to depression than others. Of course, anyone can go through periods of depression, especially if life throws them a curveball. But there are many sufferers who recognise that this tendency to depression is an aspect of their personality, and it might always be there.

So are some people just destined to be miserable?! Not at all. Many people who have a tendency to get depressed live rich and productive lives. They get to know themselves and their triggers well. They build up a 'toolbox' of coping strategies to manage the low moods, when they come.

If you are someone who often battles the blues, know that you are in good company! The pages of history are filled with people who fought this same battle, and many of them achieved incredible things in spite of it. In fact, it's often the case that those who are prone to depression are people who think deeply and care about things, which are fantastic qualities to have.

God made us all different. He gave us all different personalities, with different strengths and weaknesses. It's very tempting to look at someone else and wish we could be more like them, but that doesn't help. God chose to make you, *you*.

Who am I?

As a teenager, I didn't have a clue who I was. How could I? I spent most of my time trying to make myself into somebody else – someone I thought would be more acceptable, more accepted.

One major change was in my attitude to school work. As a younger child, I enjoyed learning and trying to do well at school. It was my habit to try my best at tasks that were set, and I glowed inside when I saw a sticker or smiley face at the end of a piece of work. But long before the end of primary school, the verdict was in: 'Rachel's a *goody-goody*.' So pronounced the most popular girl in my class. OK, so ... good was bad. Got it.

Fast forward a few years, and I was well on the way to shedding the 'good girl' image. Dyed hair, rolled up skirt, shared cigarette behind the bike sheds. Given up homework, given up *trying*. Exchanged some 'nice' friends for some, well, less nice ones.

I don't think anyone was particularly impressed. Most kids can spot a phoney a mile away. Perhaps I stopped being seen as a 'goody goody' but I never made it further than the fringes of the 'in' crowd. And frankly, I didn't belong there!

How sad that I spent so long trying to mould myself into something I wasn't, just to please other people. I know it's a familiar story. Perhaps not every young person changes their spots as quickly and often as I did, but most of us are deeply concerned about what other people think of us. We're worried that we just don't measure up. One popular song put it perfectly: 'Don't wanna be my friend no more, I wanna be somebody else!'[2]

2. Pink, 'Don't let me get me', track 2 on Missundaztood (Arista, 2001, compact disc).

Today, on my kitchen wall, there hangs a tiny wooden plaque that says this: 'In a world where you can be anything, be the person God created you to be.' When I saw it I couldn't help but think of my own journey. I want it to be a message that sinks into my children's hearts, as they grow up into young adults. One of the best things about getting older, for me, has been understanding more about who God has made me, and learning to accept that person. I'm still not there yet, but it's a journey.

I've learnt, for instance, that I'm an introvert. I love being with people, but I need time on my own to think and process things, and to recharge my batteries. I prefer being with people in small groups, or better still one-to-one, and really getting to know them. I know that my strengths lie in thinking deeply about things, in analysing books and people and situations, in building strong relationships. And I also know that these same qualities can be weaknesses. I can fall into over-thinking things, or obsessively worrying about myself and others. I can start to find my identity in what others think of me, and become easily hurt when people slight or reject me. I can be over-sensitive, irritable and moody. I'm prone to anxiety and depression.

Knowing more about our natural personality type or temperament doesn't mean we can't change or grow. If you are a Christian, there is wonderful hope for real change, and we'll talk more about that in Chapters 6 and 7. But there are some things about us that God *doesn't* change when we become Christians, and our basic temperament is one of them. I've often tried to be someone I'm not, and it just doesn't work! I will never be a loud, confident entertainer, the life and soul of the party. I'll never be a practical, DIY person or a great organiser. But that's OK; other people can be those things!

There will always be areas of our lives where we do really need God's help to change. But there are other things, like our God-given personality traits, which we can't change and don't need to. Learning to tell the difference can bring great peace and freedom.

You are fearfully and wonderfully made

In Psalm 139:13-14, David writes these words:

> For you created my inmost being;
> you knit me together in my mother's womb.
> I praise you because I am fearfully
> and wonderfully made;
> your works are wonderful
> I know that full well.

You aren't just a random collection of genes and chromosomes thrown together by chance. You are a created being, 'fearfully and wonderfully made' by a God who doesn't make mistakes. The Bible teaches us that this Creator God made mankind 'in his image', which means that we even share with God special qualities that other creatures do not have, such as our ability to reason, to choose, to create. Being made in God's image is an awe-inspiring thing; perhaps that's why David used the word 'fearfully' here. It gives every human being great dignity and worth.

All of us will have things about ourselves we don't like, things we wish we could change. And the Bible alone gives us real hope for change. If we are believers in the Lord Jesus, God promises that over time, over the course of our earthly lives, he will conform us into the image of his Son. We will become more and more like Jesus! We will become more loving, more wise, more good, more content. Free from all the insecurities and hang ups and fears that steal our joy and stop us from being the people we want to be. The change process won't be finished in this lifetime – not until we see our Saviour face to face, in Heaven, will we be made perfect. But it starts the minute we put our faith in Christ. This solid ground for hope amazed me when I first became a Christian. Time and again, I'd tried to change myself and I couldn't – but here was God promising to do just that!

Even so, if we are Christians, we should never think that God's love for us depends upon us changing. We have been adopted into his family as dearly loved children, because of what Jesus did for us on upon the cross – not because of anything we have done or can do! If you are a Christian, you are a loved and treasured child of God: 'See what great love the Father has lavished on us, that we should be called children of God! And that is what we are!' (1 John 3:1). While there may be things that God wants to change in your life, you couldn't be any more loved by him than you are right now in Christ.

Nor should you waste your time wishing you could change things about yourself that don't actually *need* changing. God doesn't completely transform our personalities, even when we become part of his family. He made you the person you are, a unique and precious individual. And who knows … it may be that the very things that make you prone to depression are things God plans to use for good purposes in your life and in the lives of others.

Something to try...

- Spend a few minutes thinking about your personality. Are you quiet, or loud, or somewhere in the middle? Shy or confident with other people? Do you tend to think about things a lot, or prefer just getting on with doing things? Do you find it more natural to listen to other people, or to talk? Be honest about your strengths and weaknesses, and jot some down if you can.

- Are there any things about yourself that you've tried to change, that might just be part of who God made you?

- Read through the whole of Psalm 139. If you feel able to pray, thank God for making you who you are, and ask him to help you to accept and appreciate that person. Pray that, over time, he will help you to change and grow into the best version of yourself that you can be, and into a person who reflects Jesus Christ.

Something to remember...

You have been 'fearfully and wonderfully made', with the unique personality that God has given you. You are precious to him.

What did Jesus say?

Are not two sparrows sold for a penny? Yet not one of them will fall to the ground outside your Father's care. And even the very hairs of your head are all numbered. So don't be afraid; you are worth more than many sparrows (Matthew 10:29-31).

WHAT HELPS?

Sometimes depression has brought me to a grinding halt.

There have been times when I couldn't muster the strength to do anything. Times when studying or working fell by the wayside. Times when I could no longer find any refuge even in familiar comforts … food, sleep, a good book.

How can you enjoy food, when depression has stolen your appetite? A good night's rest becomes a distant memory as you pass the endless night time hours lying awake, heart pounding with a nameless dread. You can't concentrate for long enough to read a book, or even follow the storyline of a film.

That's how I felt when I was sixteen and walking through the darkest months of depression I had yet faced. In fact, I wasn't walking through them at all. I was stuck. Looking back, I remember the frightening feeling that there was just no point to anything at all.

I needed medical help. That was the beginning of a long process of treatment which included a range of things, some more helpful than others.

I feel that I need to start this chapter by admitting that. I understand those crushing lows when you can't seem to do anything to help yourself. I've felt the desperation and hopelessness and fear. As you read the suggestions in this chapter, some of you might think: 'I can't. There's just no way I can possibly do any of these things.' I get that. At my lowest ebb, I couldn't either. There are times when a person needs outside help to get them to the point where they can do anything constructive to help themselves. If that is how you feel at the moment, please tell someone. Please reach out for the help you need.

I'm thankful that I was able to receive professional help at that time. I was prescribed antidepressants, and sometimes other things. I talked to people; counsellors, psychiatrists, a dietician when I wasn't eating enough. My long-suffering family had to talk to people too. It was a bumpy road, with some bumps I'd rather forget.

But fast forward a few months, and chinks of light were beginning to appear. And then a funny thing happened. As I began, slowly, to get better, I found myself beginning to make some different choices. When I could sleep again, I began to make sure I got enough of it. When I could eat again, I tried to make sure I ate (fairly) sensibly and regularly, because it seemed to make a difference. I got out of the house when I could, even if it was just going to the supermarket with my mum. I walked. I even found myself tinkling away at the piano, which I hadn't done for years. It was distracting, and as I made a bit of progress, it was satisfying. I guess I was practising what is often called 'self-care', although I didn't know it at the time. I remember finding it quite amusing, as if it was such a boring, 'old person' thing to do, to actually look after myself. To some people these things seem to come more naturally, but I had somehow forgotten how to do it.

This chapter covers some of the things I've found helpful in coping with depression, both during that time and over the years since. It's by no means an exhaustive list, and it probably won't tell you much that you haven't heard before. But don't dismiss these things out of hand. They might sound like common sense, but many of us still struggle to practise them.

Sleep

So obvious, but important! Getting enough sleep always has a big impact on how I feel, and I imagine it's the same for you. According to the experts, adults usually need 7-8 hours of sleep and teenagers even more. Of course, anxiety and depression can make getting to sleep in the first place a struggle. Or you might find that you wake up early in the morning, and can't get back to sleep. When I was severely depressed, I found that one of the hardest things to cope with.

There are lots of things that might help, like relaxing with a hot drink or having a bath, not using electronic devices too close to bedtime and reading until you feel tired. I usually try not to have caffeinated drinks too late in the day. If you are struggling with insomnia to the extent that it's affecting your ability to cope with daily life, I'd recommend talking to your doctor about it, along with your other symptoms.

Eating

It's common for those struggling with depression to overeat or under-eat. I've done both. If you have major issues with food or think you could be struggling with an eating disorder, it's really important to seek help. I have also recommended some good resources on this topic at the end of this book.

If you don't have any particular problems with eating, I'd just recommend that you try to eat regularly and *reasonably* sensibly. I won't bother telling you to lay off the junk food completely or follow some fancy diet plan. In fact, unless you're struggling with a specific weight or health issue, it's probably best not to over-think it. It's easy to get caught up in the latest nutritional trends or fad diets, but personally I haven't found it very helpful to go down that track. Just make sure you are eating three meals a day and a maybe a couple of snacks. Food does affect mood, and you won't feel good if your blood sugar is really low because you skipped breakfast, or if you're dehydrated because you're forgetting to drink.

Exercise

We all know exercise is important for our physical health, but it seems it's equally vital for our mental health. You don't have to be a top athlete, even walking will do. In fact, walking is great because it combines the benefits of moving your body with several other natural mood boosters – fresh air, being out in nature, sunlight (well, if you're lucky!). I know that when you feel really low it can be hard enough to drag yourself out of bed, let alone out for a walk. But if you possibly can, do. Maybe with a dog or a friend for company.

I'm not at all an athletic person and suffered years of ritual humiliation in school PE lessons. But over the years exercise has become an important factor in staying well. I've tried all sorts of things – aerobics, dancing, pilates, running – but generally walking has worked best for me. It may well be something different for you. Try and find something you enjoy; that way it's more likely you'll stick with it.

Hobbies

If you are in full-time education or study of some kind that takes up a lot of time and energy, which may already be in short supply if you're struggling with depression. If you have left school and are in work or looking for it – that can be exhausting too – physically and mentally. Wherever you are finding a hobby, something you do purely for fun, can be really good for your state of mind.

Other than reading, I let hobbies drop off my radar during my teens. I was so tired after school it felt like all I could do was collapse in front of the TV. But later on, when I started to exercise and play the piano again, it felt really good. As an adult I've loved learning to crochet and knit, which are a lot more fun than I would have thought! You can knit or crochet sitting still; chatting or even watching TV. Both are very calming so can be especially helpful for anxiety.

What about you? If you haven't got a hobby, are there any activities you used to enjoy that you could consider taking up again? Are there any skills you've always wanted to learn, like how to play a musical instrument or do a particular craft?

Being with people

Often when we feel depressed our instinct is to withdraw, to isolate ourselves. We do need a bit of space and alone time – especially the introverts among us. But when we're really low, it's not always good to spend too much time on our own. Negative thoughts can end up playing round and round in our minds on a never-ending loop, dragging us ever further down. Even if it's the last thing you feel like doing, you may find it helps to spend time hanging out with your family and close friends. Just doing normal, easy things, like watching TV or a film together, especially something funny, can be a welcome relief from the intensity of your own thoughts.

My younger brother Mike is four years younger than me, and as a teenage boy his vocabulary reduced right down to a series of barely audible grunts. It wasn't really surprising that he didn't have a clue what to say to his 'depressed' big sister. But one of my favourite memories was when he gruffly asked me, at a particularly low point: 'You wanna watch Gump?' (as in, the movie, *Forrest Gump*).

I did, and we did, and it was good.

Helping others

Depression can often turn us in on ourselves. Our world becomes very small. We don't mean to be selfish, but sometimes just dealing with our own emotions and making it through the day feels like more than we can cope with – let alone helping anyone else. I don't want to be heaping an extra burden of guilt on anyone here. There are certainly times when we mostly need to be on the receiving end of help.

But strangely, when we *can* find the means to help someone else, it has the double benefit of helping us too. The Bible says as much. Take Proverbs 11:25 for instance: 'A generous person will prosper; whoever refreshes others will be refreshed.' Or Acts 20:35: 'It is more blessed to give than to receive.' Of course, we should want to be kind and generous to other people just because it's the right thing to do. But it's OK that it also feels good to be able to make someone else's day just a little bit better.

It might be helping around the house, listening to a friend, reaching out to someone lonely, or something else. But when you are able, you might find that looking for opportunities to bless other people, however small they might seem, can help you too.

Getting outside

Going outside may be the last thing you feel like, but it really does help. Fresh air and sunlight are vital for mental and physical health. If you can, spend some time in quiet places where you can enjoy the natural world; the woods, the beach (if you're lucky enough to live near one), or even just your local park or green space. You may well find it lifts your spirits and gives you a new perspective on things. In fact, getting outside is so important that in certain states in the US doctors have started giving out park prescriptions to their patients!

Practising gratitude

We're probably all familiar with the old 'glass half full or half empty' analogy. The idea is that you either see the glass as half full – implying you're generally an optimist or a positive person, or half empty – implying you're more pessimistic or negative. It's not quite as simple as that of course; most of us can be both, at different times. But it is easy to drift into patterns of negative thinking, where we always see what's *wrong* with a situation. We're always aware of what we lack, and forget to appreciate what we have. There is much to be said for the simple practice of 'counting our blessings'.

Often this doesn't come naturally; it certainly doesn't to me. If I was a character in Winnie-the-Pooh, I'm sorry to say I'd probably be Eeyore, the gloomy donkey! But at times when I have made a deliberate effort to list things to be thankful for, I've found it does make a difference. Today even non-Christian counsellors often recommend keeping a 'gratitude journal' in which you might try to write down just three things a day to be thankful for. If you are a Christian, the wonderful thing is that you have someone to be thankful *to*!

'Every good and perfect gift is from above ...' (James 1:17).

Remember, you don't have to *feel* thankful to give thanks. But you may find that as you think intentionally about the good things in your life, your feelings begin to follow.

Professional help

If you do visit the doctor to seek help for your depression, which I would strongly recommend, there are a couple of things they might offer.

Depending partly on your age, you may be offered medication, such as antidepressant tablets. This will most likely be a type of antidepressant called an SSRI (Selective Serotonin Reuptake Inhibiter). Whether or not this is a good treatment option for you is something that you and your parents or caregivers need to consider together under proper medical advice. Doctors are usually cautious about prescribing mood-altering drugs to young people, and will only consider this in the case of moderate to severe depression.

Antidepressants are certainly a helpful aspect of treatment for some people, although they are not a cure. Often people testify that when they were severely depressed, medication helped them to get to a point where they could try other things to tackle some of the deeper issues in their lives, maybe through talking therapies (see below). Or just to be well enough that they could practise some of the lifestyle strategies talked about in this chapter. Others are determined not to go down the medication route, and that is their choice. Antidepressants are not the only treatment option for depression, and may not always be the best one.

If you *are* prescribed antidepressants, be aware that it will always take a little while for these to have a positive effect, and that there may be side effects in the first couple of weeks. Try to stick with the treatment for long enough to allow it to work. In most cases the side effects should subside as your body gets used to it. Often people do find that they get worse before they begin to get better. Your doctor should be monitoring you closely during the early days and weeks of taking an antidepressant.

You may also be offered some sort of counselling, or talking therapy. One kind of therapy that has been proven to have positive results over recent years is CBT (Cognitive Behaviour Therapy). CBT is more practical than some other kinds of counselling and really suits some people. It involves identifying some of the patterns of thinking that make you feel bad, and gently challenging those where necessary. CBT or another type of therapy may be suggested to you, but it may be that your parents or carers need to pay for it privately. If you and they decide together this is something you would like to try, make sure you get a recommendation from your doctor of a trusted therapist. If you are a Christian, you will also want to explain that to any therapist or counsellor you start working with. Be honest if any ideas come up that don't seem to be in line with what the Bible teaches. A good therapist should be happy to help you consider things in the light of your Christian faith.

It is also worth mentioning Biblical Counselling. This is a branch of Christian counselling that has been gaining ground in recent decades, particularly in the US but more recently in the UK as well. There are many excellent resources available that help to apply the Bible's wisdom more specifically to mental health struggles, and I have included some recommendations at the back of this book. It is not always easy to find a trained biblical counsellor in the UK, but if you go to church it is certainly worth speaking with your minister or another church leader about it. They may be able to point you in the right direction, or perhaps suggest some other form of Christian counselling.

What if I can't do anything?

At the beginning of the chapter, I confessed that there have been times in my life when I've found it almost impossible to do things – even good things – to help myself. If you are currently in the grip of severe depression, perhaps some of the suggestions in this chapter seem completely beyond you at the moment.

Please don't worry. Rest assured, these are not boxes to tick or tasks you must complete. They are not more things to beat yourself up about not doing. They are simply habits that can help. If they are beyond you at the moment, set them aside for now. Perhaps there will be a time for some of them later on, when those chinks of light begin to appear.

God our helper

Many of the Psalms speak of God as a helper. In Psalm 63, for instance, David prays:

> Because you are my help,
> I sing in the shadow of your wings.
> I cling to you;
> your right hand upholds me.
> (Psalm 63:7-8)

In Psalm 70:

> But as for me, I am poor and needy;
> come quickly to me, O God.
> You are my help and my deliverer;
> LORD, do not delay.
> (Psalm 70:5)

God is the ultimate helper. He made us, he knows us inside and out, and he loves us more than we can comprehend. He is both *willing* and *able* to help us. Willing, because of his great love; able, because of his mighty power.

The Psalms show us how to cry out to him for help; admitting our need, not pretending to be OK when we're not. Of course, God knows how we really feel anyway. But he wants to teach us to look to him for help. He longs for us to recognise him as the one who can provide it.

Looking to God for help doesn't mean ignoring other kinds of help, such as those we have talked about in this chapter. God often works *through* these things to help us. Food, sleep and exercise, nature and friendship ... these are all his gifts to us, his blessings. Help from God comes in many forms, some of them very ordinary seeming.

But for the Christian believer, there is more help available. The Bible tells us that 'man does not live on bread alone, but on every word that comes from the mouth of God' (Matthew 4:4). Psalm 119, the longest Psalm in the Bible, tells us more about that Word, the Word of God. It is really a love song, a song that expresses the deep joy and delight the Psalmist feels for God's words:

> I rejoice in following your statutes, as one rejoices in great riches (verse 14).

My soul is consumed with longing for your laws at all times (verse 20).

Your statutes are my delight; they are my counsellors (verse 24).

My soul is weary with sorrow; strengthen me according to your word (verse 28).

My soul faints with longing for your salvation, but I have put my hope in your word (verse 81).

Your word is a lamp for my feet, a light on my path (verse 105).

In giving us his Word, the Bible, God has given us a rich treasure trove of wisdom, truth and light. It is in the Bible that God reveals himself to us – who he is, what he's done, why it matters. And it is in the Bible that we begin to see ourselves more clearly. We begin to understand why life can be such a struggle, and we are pointed towards the best help that is available.

Something to try…

- Make a list of some of the things that help you to feel better when you're in the grip of depression. I know sometimes the answer might be 'nothing' – but think hard. Try to remember times when something has helped to distract you or gradually draw you out of a low place.

- Look back over the suggestions in this chapter. Are there any in particular you know you are neglecting, like exercise, eating well or getting enough sleep? Think about any small changes you could make to give yourself the best chance to feel well.

Something to remember...

God is the ultimate helper. He is both willing and able to help us, if we ask him.

What did Jesus say?

'Everyone who hears these words of mine and puts them into practice is like a wise man who built his house on the rock. The rain came down, the streams rose, and the winds blew and beat against that house; yet it did not fall, because it had its foundation on the rock' (Matthew 7:24-25).

WHAT HURTS?

Your sister's, like, the thinnest person I've ever seen!'

I wasn't supposed to hear that, but I did, and I glowed inside. I don't think that it was meant as a compliment, but I took it as one anyway. The last few weeks had been pretty grim, but losing my appetite at least had one happy result. As I'd noticed the pounds dropping off, I thought I'd carry on that way. I started hiding food in my wardrobe. I hadn't set out to lose weight, but I wasn't complaining.

Anyway, this weekend was going to be different; a welcome change. I was visiting my older sister at University. New people, new places, a night out to look forward to. I could be anyone I wanted to be. I looked fine on the outside; no one knew how fragile I was on the inside.

With a group of her friends, we went from student bar to student bar, drinking and dancing. I might have been the little sister, but I was in my element. I was already well acquainted with alcohol and we were on good terms. I loved the effect it had on me, filling me with the confidence to crack jokes and flirt with strangers. Taking me away from the sadness and emptiness in my own head.

For a while. Hours later, we were back at the student halls. I sat in my sister's small bedroom alone, listening to her arguing with her boyfriend outside.

The evening was over and I suddenly felt desperate. It hadn't changed anything, and tomorrow I'd be going back to reality. I couldn't escape myself, or the mess my life was in.

Do as I say, not as I do?

I made some pretty bad choices in my teens. I don't know how much these bad choices contributed to my depression, or how much they were a result of it. Like the chicken and the egg, it's hard to say which came first!

In the last chapter we looked at some of the things that can help in the battle with depression. In this one, we're going to look at some of the things that really don't help, and will probably make it worse. Again, it's not a complete list, but just a place to start.

Also, please don't read this as a lecture. I know you will make your own choices. I did; often in spite of what my parents or any other adult advised me! It was a slow process to make the link between some of my habits and how bad I felt. And even as I began to recognise some of the things that were hurting instead of helping, I didn't always find it easy to choose differently.

Overthinking

Thinking is part of being human and certainly not a bad thing. Without thinking we can't learn, we can't plan, we can't understand, we can't recognise problems and find solutions. But many of us, myself included, tend to *overthink.* We mull over certain things endlessly in our minds and obsess about them. It might be a particular relationship, or a problem at school, or a future event we're worried about. Sometimes we do this because we mistakenly believe that the more we think over this problem, the more likely we are to come up with a solution. Instead, we often find that anxiety paralyses us. Because we've thought about something for so long, we can no longer see the basic facts clearly. The thing we're thinking about may have become much bigger in our minds than it really needs to be.

If, like me, this is something you struggle with, try to get into the habit of recognising when you're overthinking about something, and change the record. Go out, do something, watch TV even. If there is a problem you genuinely need to think about, you can always come back to it later. Some people even suggest scheduling a designated 'worry time'. I've never tried it, but if it helps you get on with the rest of your day then why not!

Drugs & alcohol

Experimenting with drugs and alcohol is a temptation for many young people, and it is the stage of life when we are most likely to take risks. For those who suffer from depression, the relief or distraction of drink or drugs might seem particularly appealing. If you feel terrible, why wouldn't you want to try something that might make you feel better, or at least different? After all, what have you got to lose? That was my thinking, anyway.

However, drugs and depression aren't a great combination – to say the least. A few beers or a joint might offer temporary relief, but you're likely to feel much worse in the long run. While the effects of the drug are wearing off, whether it's a hangover or a 'come down' from an illegal high, you'll often feel anxious and agitated, or moody and flat. If you experiment with drugs while you are suffering from depression, you are much more likely to make bad decisions and cause yourself harm.

During my lowest months, I was willing to try almost anything to feel different. Thankfully, it didn't take me too long to realise that drugs were no good for me. It was harder with alcohol. It was so much a part of the world I inhabited back then.

In hindsight, I should have rethought my relationship with alcohol much sooner. Leaning on alcohol to 'fix' things doesn't work; for one thing, it adds as many problems as it seems to solve, and for another, it slows down the process of finding the things that really do help.

Self-harm

Self-harm is a term that describes any kind of deliberate attempt to hurt yourself, whether it's through an eating disorder, drug or alcohol abuse, or inflicting physical pain through cutting, pinching or burning yourself. I spent several years wearing long sleeves ... even in summer.

Statistics suggest that increasing numbers of young people are turning to self-harm as a way of dealing with their overwhelming emotions. Sometimes when you have intense feelings swirling around inside you, it's hard to know what to do with them. You long for an outlet, a way to express them, to get them out ... but how? Self-harm can seem to offer a release, of sorts.

We've already looked at how changes in the teenage brain result in greater extremes of emotion. Feelings really are more intense at this time in our lives, and yet the part of our brain that helps us decide how best to respond to those feelings, the prefrontal cortex, is still developing. This doesn't mean, of course, that adults always deal with their emotions rationally or well – far from it! But it does mean that for teenagers, the struggle to manage strong emotions can be especially tough.

There are lots of other, positive ways we can try to process out-of-control emotions: writing, music, drawing, a brisk walk, a run, talking to other people, talking to God. Like drugs or alcohol, self-harm can seem to offer a quick fix of sorts but it is never the answer. If you are harming yourself at the moment, PLEASE tell somebody and ask for help.

Social media & screens

Digital technology is developing fast. I didn't have an email account or a mobile phone until I was nineteen, and when I was a teenager social media didn't even exist! If it had, I'm sure I would have jumped on board with enthusiasm, but I'm equally sure it would have made my life more complicated.

Of course, social media isn't all bad; it can be a great way to connect with people and to keep in touch, but it can also lead to feelings of insecurity and inadequacy. We are constantly bombarded with images of people who seem to look better, feel better and do better at everything than we do. We're constantly aware of parties we weren't invited to and friendships that don't include us. Worse still, we can become so immersed in our on-screen lives that we're less connected with our real lives. Messaging, 'liking' posts and comparing photos is no replacement for real friendships in real time!

Several studies have looked into the relationship between social media use and depression, although it's hard to confirm a link. For one thing, it's hard to tell whether excessive social media use leads to depression, because those who suffer from depression are probably more likely to spend a lot of time online. However, it's well worth doing your own research – how do you feel after a long session online? Or half an hour scrolling through your Snapchat or Instagram feed? Do you feel better or worse? I find that sometimes it's simply compulsive; I don't know why I'm doing it and I'm not even enjoying it.

It's unrealistic to suggest that you give up watching box sets or messaging your friends, and I wouldn't dream of it! But you might want to think a bit about the effect that your screen time has on you, and try to keep things in balance.

Peer pressure

Friendships are really important. But if we're honest, some friendships are more helpful than others. In the Bible, the writer of the book of Proverbs puts it quite bluntly: 'Walk with the wise and become wise, for a companion of fools suffers harm' (Proverbs 13:20).

When I was a teenager, certain friends had a huge influence on me, and it wasn't always for good. I can't blame them for everything that went wrong in my life – I wasn't a great influence on them either! But I often wish that

I had been a bit more discerning about the people I chose to get close to.

Tread carefully in friendships with others who struggle with mental health issues. It may be that you can be of great support to one another, but sometimes this kind of friendship can be very intense emotionally. Supporting someone with depression can be hard and draining. Although you won't want to hurt anyone's feelings, there may be times when a bit of healthy distance is needed. If this is an issue for you, it would be well worth talking to a parent or other adult about it and asking for their advice.

It can be the case that young people even influence one another towards self-harm, eating disorders etc, especially on social media. If you're affected by anything like this, *please* talk to an adult about it.

Inaction

For many people, depression can bring on a kind of paralysis. Everything feels so hard –

getting out of bed, getting dressed, performing even basic daily tasks – let alone going to school or work. 'Tiredness' always comes high up on the lists of depression symptoms, and many depression sufferers retreat to the bedroom or the sofa when they're struggling the most.

This is especially hard when your depression is moderate to severe. There will probably be times – maybe a lot of times – when you simply can't do what people would normally expect of you, or what you expect of yourself. It can be one of the toughest things about living with depression. I don't want to pile extra guilt on anybody, especially those who are currently struggling with severe depression.

But I also know that when my depression is milder, there are times when I need to push myself a bit. Long periods of lying around doing nothing don't tend to make anyone feel better. I can end up in a vicious circle – I'm depressed so I do nothing, but doing nothing makes me feel useless and rubbish, so then I feel even more depressed and even less able to get up and do anything!

So whenever you can, do something. Have a shower. Go to school. Meet a friend. Go for a walk. Help with the washing up. Whatever it is ... just 'do the next thing'. There's a well-known poem with that title which you can find in full at the back of this book. During one difficult time I wrote it out and stuck it up on a kitchen cupboard etc.

More recently, a similar phrase has been popularised in the film *Frozen 2*:

Take a step, step again
It is all that I can do
The next right thing

I won't look too far ahead
It's too much for me to take
But break it down to this next breath, this next step
This next choice is one that I can make
So I'll walk through this night
Stumbling blindly toward the light
And do the next right thing ...[1]

---

1. https://genius.com/Kristen-bell-the-next-right-thing-lyrics

OK, I may be quoting the words of a Disney character, but it's good advice!

True strength

One thing Anna didn't have in the movie (or at least she didn't mention it), was help from a source much higher and greater than herself. Often popular culture urges us to 'search for the hero inside yourself' – but this message couldn't be more different from what the Bible says. In fact, Jesus said to his followers: 'Apart from me you can do nothing'! (John 15:5)

The world sets a high value on being 'strong'. We tend to look up to those we see as being strong, who have it all together, who are independent and don't ever seem to struggle or need help with anything. The Bible turns all of that on its head. True strength isn't shown by pretending we don't need anyone; it's shown by admitting that we do. As human beings, the truth is that we aren't actually independent! We depend even for our next breath on the God who created us.

In Psalm 61, David prays:

> From the ends of the earth I call to you,
> I call as my heart grows faint;
> lead me to the rock that is higher than I.
> For you have been my refuge,
> a strong tower against the foe.
> (Psalm 61:2-3)

God is the one who is strong. He is a rock, a refuge, a strong tower. And he gladly offers help and protection to those who would call out to him.

Many of the things that hurt us when we have depression are things we have turned to looking for comfort or distraction. But they offer a false hope. Instead of making things better, in the long run they make them worse.

Not so with God. He is strong, he is able, and he will help us in exactly the way we need.

> Praise be to the LORD,
> for he has heard my cry for mercy.
> The LORD is my strength and my shield;
> my heart trusts in him, and he helps me.
> My heart leaps for joy,
> and with my song I praise him
> (Psalm 28:6-7)

Something to try...

- Think about the things you most often turn to for help when you are depressed. If you are being honest with yourself, do any of them cause more harm than good? If you aren't sure, think about the things listed in this chapter as a starting point.

Something to remember...

We often look for 'quick fixes' to our problems, but God offers help that is real and lasting.

What did Jesus say?

'Peace I leave with you; my peace I give you. I do not give to you as the world gives. Do not let your hearts be troubled and do not be afraid' (John 14:27).

WHAT HEALS? (PART 1)

I didn't turn to God for help when I was depressed.

That might seem strange, since I had grown up in a Christian family. I even prayed a special prayer as a little girl, asking God into my life. I certainly understood something about Jesus, and once thought I loved him. I knew it upset me when children at school said they didn't believe in God. Or when a visiting cousin stared scornfully at the Bible verses Mum had stuck up in my room. 'Why have you got so many *God* posters on your walls?'

But really, the most important thing in my life was to be accepted, to fit in, to be liked. As I grew older, it soon became obvious that being a Christian wasn't going to help me much with any of those goals. So it had to go. Not overnight, but gradually, bit by bit, the small, faltering faith that I'd once had eroded away.

And then, even when things began to go really wrong in my life, I'm not sure it occurred to me to ask God for help. By then I was so used to being on my own. I don't think I really thought of him at all anymore.

I was nineteen when that changed. It was my first morning at University, after Mum and Dad had helped me move my stuff in the previous day.

Knowing no one, I found myself heading to a meeting I'd seen advertised on a poster, a breakfast hosted by the college Christian Union. I guess I assumed that Christians would have to be nice to me, and just then I needed nice! But I felt horribly out of place as the girls around me chatted about which churches to try. I hadn't been to church in years, except maybe at Christmas. I couldn't wait to make my excuses and leave.

For a few weeks, that was that. But then, a girl on my course invited me to come along with her to a meeting for people investigating the Christian faith. *I* wasn't investigating the Christian faith. I'm not at all sure why I went, unless it was the prospect of free food! But it was the beginning of a journey that led me, at last, back to God. The God I'd turned away from but who, wonderfully, had never turned away from me.

Good News

So what did I hear at that meeting, and the others that followed? And why did it suddenly make sense to me, then, in a way that it never had before?

I heard about a God who had made the world and everything in it, including me.

You are worthy, our Lord and God, to receive glory and honour and power, for you created all things, and by your will they were created and have their being (Revelation 4:11).

I heard about how all of us had rejected him, and tried to live our lives our own way without him. Including me.

There is no one righteous, not even one;
there is no one who understands; there is no one
who seeks God. All have turned away
(Romans 3:10-12).

I heard about how that God is a holy God, a just and perfect God, who must punish sin and evil. I heard how, because of our rejection of him, because of that one great sin and everything that follows it, we are all heading for death and judgement. Including me.

People are destined to die once, and after
that to face judgment
(Hebrews 9:27).

But after that bad news, *very* bad news, I heard the good news. I heard about how God loves us so much that he has provided a way out. How he sent a rescuer, his beloved son, Jesus Christ, to die in our place, taking our punishment through his death on the cross so that people can be forgiven. Even me.

For Christ also suffered once for sins, the righteous
for the unrighteous, to bring you to God
(1 Peter 3:18).

And I heard about how, wonderfully, death was not the end for Jesus, but how he rose from the grave three days later, to be our Lord and Saviour and friend for ever.

I heard about how, through his death and resurrection, we too can have a life beyond this one. A life that is full and rich and joyful beyond our imagining. Free, and forgiven, with everything made new. Even for me!

Praise be to the God and Father of our Lord Jesus
Christ! In his great mercy he has given us new birth
into a living hope through the resurrection of Jesus
Christ from the dead, and into an inheritance
that can never perish, spoil or fade
(1 Peter 1:3-4).[1]

That is the gospel, the 'good news' about Jesus, that I heard. It is both wonderfully simple, and mind-bogglingly complex! I had heard it before, but the years away had brought confusion and doubt. I had many questions.

---

1. Structure and verses borrowed from Philip Jenson & Tony Payne, *Two Ways to Live* (Matthias Media, 2004)

There was a lot of talking, and reading, and thinking, and praying, before I finally came to believe that this good news was true, and asked Jesus to come into my life.

I soon realised what had been missing before. I had never known God personally. I had known some stuff about him, but I hadn't *known* him. Now I experienced the thrill of hearing him speak to me through the pages of Scripture. I was a student of literature, so books were what I lived and breathed, and yet in the Bible I discovered a book like no other. Now that I knew a little of life, I saw that the Bible explained it like nothing else could. Now that I knew a little of human nature, I saw how the Bible explained *me* like nothing else could. I knew that God was speaking to me personally through his Word, and I could speak back to him in prayer. A relationship had begun.

Jesus came not for the healthy, but for the sick

When I began to listen to Christians teaching the Bible, one of the first things that struck me was that according to them, I was not okay.

What a relief! Because if there was one thing those last few years had taught me, it was that. *I was definitely not okay.* But according to the Bible, no one was. There was something terribly wrong with all of us. Until we see that, the Christian message doesn't make a whole lot of sense. The good news, that Jesus came to die for us so that we can be forgiven, is only good news to those who have accepted the bad news – that there is something that needs forgiving. And not just a little thing, that could be shrugged off or swept under the carpet. Our sin against God matters enough that it took Jesus' death to put it right.

During Jesus' time on earth he often spent time with people the rest of Jewish society looked down on, like prostitutes and tax collectors. The religious leaders held that against him, and asked his disciples: 'Why does he eat with tax collectors and sinners?'

> Jesus answered: 'It is not the healthy who need a doctor, but those who are ill. I have not come to call the righteous, but sinners'
> (Mark 2:17).

Jesus didn't come for people who thought they had it all together. He came for people with problems and needs. People who struggled, who messed up, who got things wrong. People just like you and me.

Is depression 'sin'?

Christians with depression often wonder if it is just a spiritual issue. Sometimes other Christians might imply that depression is just sin. Maybe we're just drowning in self-pity. Maybe we're just not trusting God enough.

There are other people who think depression has nothing to do with our spiritual lives. It's just the same as any physical illness or injury – like having a broken arm. It's a medical problem with medical solutions.

In my experience, both these positions can be unhelpful. I'm neither a doctor nor a pastor, but I think the picture is far more complex. Scientific research would seem to suggest that there *are* physiological factors involved in depression, perhaps related to the balance of chemicals in the brain. It seems likely that there are genetic factors involved as well, but there is still much we don't understand. It's not at all clear medically why some people suffer from depression and others don't.

On the other hand, the Bible is clear that we are all sinners. Even Christians. 'If we claim to be without sin, we deceive ourselves and the truth is not in us,' wrote the apostle John (1 John 1:8). I know that I am prone to depression, and that doesn't make me any more sinful than anyone else. But I've found that I can certainly react to my depression in sinful ways, which might even prolong it or make it worse.

Depression involves both sin *and* sickness. Only God fully understands where one ends and the other begins! We need to be careful not to judge other people, because we don't know their hearts or what they are going through. If a Christian believer is struggling with depression, we shouldn't assume that there's a problem with their faith. We need to pray, both for ourselves and for others who struggle, that God would help us to see our hearts more clearly. We can ask that he will help us to stop feeling guilty about things that are not our fault. But we should also pray that he would show us where things *are* wrong in our hearts, so that we can repent and move forwards. 'If we confess our sins, he is faithful and just and will forgive us our sins and purify us from all unrighteousness.' (1 John 1:9)

Confession

Psalm 51 is a Psalm of heartfelt confession. We are told when David wrote it, after an incident that was surely one of the low points of his life. While his armies were away fighting in battle, King David was lounging around at home in the palace when he set eyes on a beautiful woman named Bathsheba from his rooftop. In spite of the fact that she was married, and her husband was a soldier away risking his life for David's army, the King summoned her and committed adultery with her. Even worse, when Bathsheba became pregnant and David's attempt to cover things up didn't work, he orchestrated things so that her husband Uriah would be killed in battle, before taking Bathsheba to be his own wife!

It's a shocking story, which you can read for yourself in 2 Samuel, chapters 11 and 12. And the man who did these things was the same David who was once described as being a man after God's own heart! But the very fact that we find this story in our Bibles gives us hope. If there are things you have done – or thought, or said – that you are ashamed of, take comfort in this. Whatever wrong things you have done, God is ready and willing to forgive you.

Read the words of Psalm 51, below. You could consider using the words of this Psalm as a personal prayer of confession, which is something I have often found helpful.

Psalm 51

For the director of music. A psalm of David. When the prophet Nathan came to him after David had committed adultery with Bathsheba.

Have mercy on me, O God,
according to your unfailing love;
according to your great compassion
blot out my transgressions.
Wash away all my iniquity
and cleanse me from my sin.
For I know my transgressions,
and my sin is always before me.
Against you, you only, have I sinned
and done what is evil in your sight;
so you are right in your verdict
and justified when you judge.
Surely I was sinful at birth,
sinful from the time my mother conceived me.
Yet you desired faithfulness even in the womb;
you taught me wisdom in that secret place.
Cleanse me with hyssop, and I will be clean;
wash me, and I will be whiter than snow.
Let me hear joy and gladness;
let the bones you have crushed rejoice.
Hide your face from my sins
and blot out all my iniquity.
Create in me a pure heart, O God,
and renew a steadfast spirit within me.
Do not cast me from your presence

or take your Holy Spirit from me.
Restore to me the joy of your salvation
and grant me a willing spirit, to sustain me.
Then I will teach transgressors your ways,
so that sinners will turn back to you.
Deliver me from the guilt of bloodshed, O God,
you who are God my Saviour,
and my tongue will sing of your righteousness.
Open my lips, Lord,
and my mouth will declare your praise.
You do not delight in sacrifice, or I would bring it;
you do not take pleasure in burnt offerings.
My sacrifice, O God, is a broken spirit;
a broken and contrite heart
you, God, will not despise.
May it please you to prosper Zion,
to build up the walls of Jerusalem.
Then you will delight in the sacrifices of the
righteous,
in burnt offerings offered whole;
then bulls will be offered on your altar.

Forgiveness

When we have felt the full weight of our sin,
finding that Jesus has taken the punishment
we deserve is good news indeed. When we
have grieved over the state of our hearts, the
promise of forgiveness brings great comfort
and joy.

For as high as the heavens are above the earth,
so great is his love for those who fear him;
as far as the east is from the west,
so far has he removed our transgressions
from us
(Psalm 103:11-12).

Wow! How incredible to have my sins – all the wrong things I have thought and said and done – taken far, far away from me. Elsewhere the Bible uses several other powerful images to illustrate this wonderful truth. Read these slowly and let them really sink in:

I have swept away your offences like a cloud,
your sins like the morning mist
(Isaiah 44:22).

Though your sins are like scarlet,
they shall be as white as snow;
though they are red as crimson,
they shall be like wool
(Isaiah 1:18).

You will again have compassion on us;
you will tread our sins underfoot
and hurl all our iniquities
into the depths of the sea
(Micah 7:19).

From sorrow to praise

It is natural for forgiven sinners to praise God. The Psalms give voice to our sorrow and grief, our crying out to God in pain – but they also overflow with praise:

> Praise the LORD, my soul;
> all my inmost being, praise his holy name.
> Praise the LORD, my soul,
> and forget not all his benefits -
> who forgives all your sins
> and heals all your diseases,
> who redeems your life from the pit
> and crowns you with love and compassion,
> who satisfies your desires with good things
> so that your youth is renewed like the eagle's
> (Psalm 103:1-5).

This Psalm meant a lot to me as a new believer. I saw it on a poster in a Christian bookstore and stuck it up on the wall of my college bedroom. I felt that depression had stolen so much of my teenage years, but this promise was sweet to my ears. God alone could redeem my life from the pit, renew my youth and satisfy me with good things. He has done all that and more, more than I could ask or imagine!

But praise doesn't always come easily, even after many years of following Jesus. Often I am too caught up in my own problems, and too preoccupied with what I don't have, to remember God's goodness. In the words of the Psalm, I do 'forget all his benefits.' I need to be deliberate, to keep reminding myself of all that God has done in my life. I need to keep reminding myself how different it is to what I really deserve.

Depression turns us inward. Praise forces us to turn upward and outward, to look away from ourselves and look instead to God. It feels hard at first, unnatural. But it's essential to human happiness. We can never find true joy when we believe the world is all about us. Only God is enough to satisfy our longings and fill our emptiness.

Something to try...

- If you wouldn't call yourself a Christian, or if you aren't sure, why not give some time to investigating the Christian faith? It would be a great idea to start by reading through one of the gospel accounts of Jesus' life in the Bible, such as the book of Mark or Luke. At the back of this book there are also some titles of other recommended books that can help you find out more about what Christians believe and why.

- If you are a Christian, read and pray through Psalm 103. Think particularly about sins you need to confess, and then draw comfort from God's promise that 'as far as the east is from the west, so far has he removed our transgressions from us.' Use the words of this Psalm to praise and thank God for his mercy.

Something to remember...

If you have put your trust in Jesus and his death on the cross, your sins are forgiven. You have new life in Christ, and a sure and certain hope that can never be taken away.

What did Jesus say?

Very truly I tell you, whoever hears my word and believes him who sent me has eternal life and will not be judged but has crossed over from death to life (John 5:24).

WHAT HEALS? (PART 2)

It was a beautiful day in early May.

It was warm enough to sit out on the patio at my parents' house, as I stared at the interplay of light and shadow on the lawn under the walnut tree.

There was an old hymn book open on my lap and I scoured its pages for words that might comfort, that might heal. 'When morning gilds the skies,' I whispered, 'My heart awaking cries ... may Jesus Christ be praised!' Silent tears slid down my cheeks and dripped onto the page.

I wasn't supposed to be here.

The university term wasn't over. All my friends were still at college, immersed in frantic revision for our second year exams, just a few weeks away. At the moment, I didn't know whether or not I would even be taking those exams. Neither did my supervisor. A week earlier I had visited his office to tell him that I needed to go home.

Only those closest to me knew what a miracle it was that I had made it to university at all. Depression had left its mark on my academic record, but over the last few years I'd worked hard to make up for it. Now it looked as though that hard work might come to nothing after all. I was going to throw it all away, mess everything up ... again.

When I'd become a Christian, I thought that my struggles with depression were over. In my mind there was a clear link between turning away from God in my early teens and the descent into depression. Without God in my life, there had been no point to anything. I'd had no purpose and no hope.

But now that I was a *Christian*, all that had wonderfully changed! I had a relationship with the supremely good, powerful and loving God, my Father, my Saviour, my best friend. I had a purpose – to live for him, to tell others about him and to grow more and more like him. And I had a sure and certain hope, that one day I would live forever with him in Heaven. Things were going to be very different now!

And in a lot of ways, they had been. My lifestyle had changed. My hobbies had changed. My friends had changed. I began to care less about some things that had worried me for years, like my weight, my looks, what other people thought of me. And I began to care more about other things, like becoming part of a church family, getting to know the Bible better, and trying to tell other people about Jesus, so that they too could know the peace and freedom I had found in him.

But obviously I'd been wrong to think that depression would remain safely in my past. Because here I was. I felt confused, a failure.

What had gone wrong? I was a Christian; I should be happy. Surely I had every reason to be happy!

There was so much about the life of faith that I had yet to learn.

The truth is that even when we become Christians, we aren't blessed with a pain-free, trouble-free life. We still live in a fallen world, a broken world. We're still sinners; forgiven sinners, changing sinners, but sinners all the same. Our hope of perfection lies beyond this earthly life. Here, now, we still mess things up. We still hurt other people. We still hurt ourselves.

I was a new creation ... but I was also still myself. And my problems hadn't disappeared. I was still prone to depression and anxiety. They weren't always there, but they hovered close at hand. They seemed to follow me like ominous black clouds, ever on the verge of breaking into thunder and showers.

What difference does it make?

As a young Christian, I was left with a big question to grapple with. I knew the gospel, the good news about Jesus and his death for me upon the cross. I knew that I was forgiven. I knew that I had a wonderful future to look forward to, the promise of eternal life to come.

But what difference did all this make to me, that day in my parents' back garden? Or the next day, or the day after that? What difference did it make when I felt stuck, unable to cope any more with the demands of daily life? What difference did it make when my thoughts were consumed with fears and worries I couldn't articulate? What difference did it make when I knew the truth but still felt overwhelmed with emptiness, and had no idea why?

We were made for relationship

The Bible tells us that God created us to be in a relationship with him. In the very first book of the Bible, the book of Genesis, Adam and

125

Eve enjoy that relationship fully in the garden of Eden. God walks with them and talks with them. But that's before sin enters the world and destroys that special relationship. Satan, in the form of a snake, sows seeds of doubt in Eve's heart about God. Can his words really be trusted? Does he really want what's best for her? Or is he just a killjoy, who wants to deprive her of pleasure and fulfilment?

When Adam and Eve disobeyed God, sin ruined mankind's relationship with him. And it has done so ever since. Now we come into the world under the curse of sin and wonder why things don't feel quite right. On the one hand there's so much that is good in our lives. There are people to love and pleasures to enjoy. But there's also so much brokenness. Relationships that are strained or shattered beyond repair. Longings that remain unsatisfied. Hopes that are dashed. Opportunities that are wasted. Aware of this tension, we grow up feeling confused, conflicted and strangely alone.

When I suffered from depression as a teenager, I felt lonelier than I'd ever felt before. In fact, I think it's fair to say that loneliness is one of the hardest things about struggling with mental health issues. As the book of Proverbs puts it: 'Each heart knows its own bitterness.' No one else really knows the pain we are in. No one else can truly understand what we're going through.

Well, not quite no one. God does understand. In fact, as we saw earlier in Psalm 139, there is nothing we can hide from him – even if we want to. God made us, he sees everything that happens to us, he knows how it makes us feel. He knows how we're wired. He understands, better than anyone else ever could.

The Bible tells us that this God who made us still wants to have a relationship with us. He designed us to be in relationship with him, and he knows we cannot thrive without it.

One of the verses that describes this most vividly is in the last book of the Bible, the book of Revelation. It pictures Jesus, literally knocking at the door of our hearts, asking to be let in:

> 'Here I am!' he says.
> 'I stand at the door and knock.
> If anyone hears my voice and opens the door,
> I will come in and eat with that person,
> and they with me'
> (Revelation 3:20).

Our relationship with God was well and truly broken. Jesus was the only one who could repair it, and he came down to earth to do just that. He died on the cross to take the punishment for our sin so that we can be forgiven. If we put our trust in Jesus, we can be friends with God.

But what does that relationship look like, day to day? What does it mean to let Jesus in, and eat with him? And how does it help us, when we still live in a fallen world, where things are often painful and hard?

We can know Jesus now

Unlike Jesus' first followers, we can't talk with him face to face. We can't literally walk beside him, listen to his words, or hold his hand. But we can still have a relationship with him that is every bit as real. Before his death and resurrection, Jesus told his disciples how – it would be through the Holy Spirit:

> I will ask the Father, and he will give
> you another advocate to help you
> and be with you for ever – the Spirit of truth.
> The world cannot accept him,
> because it neither sees him nor knows him.
> But you know him,
> for he lives with you and will be in you.
> I will not leave you as orphans; I will come to you
> (John 14:16-18).

Those who invite Jesus into their lives know his presence with them through the Holy Spirit. Every Christian believer has the Spirit living in them, not just a privileged few. In fact the apostle Paul tells us that 'no one can say "Jesus is Lord" except by the Holy Spirit' (1 Corinthians 12:3).

And although we can't see our Saviour in the flesh like the first disciples did, Jesus makes it clear that this isn't second best.

When 'doubting' Thomas touched his scars, Jesus said:

> Because you have seen me,
> you have believed;
> blessed are those who have
> not seen and yet have believed
> (John 20:29).

We can listen to Jesus speak to us now through the words of the Bible. As we read his words, the Spirit who lives in us helps us to understand. He guides us to the words we really need to hear, when we most need to hear them. He speaks to us, convicts us, guides us and changes us.

The Holy Spirit also helps us to pray. If you are struggling with depression at the moment, it may be that you're finding it hard to pray. I can't tell you how often my own prayers have been nothing more than a simple, 'Help me!' But even when we can't find the words nor the will to pray, the Spirit steps in to speak for us.

> The Spirit helps us in our weakness.
> For we do not know what to pray for as we ought,
> but the Spirit himself intercedes
> for us with groanings too deep for words
> (Romans 8:26, ESV).

130

Jesus knows our struggles

God understands our pain and our weakness because he made us and knows us inside out. But he also understands because in Jesus, he entered our world and became a man. In the gospel accounts of Jesus' life, we see that he grew hungry, and thirsty. He knew what it was to be exhausted. He felt grief over suffering and death, and he wept. But his sorrows went further. He was humiliated, rejected even by his closest friends. He was mocked and despised. He was beaten. He was killed.

The writer of the Book of Hebrews explains why this should bring us great comfort:

For we do not have a high priest
who is unable to feel sympathy
for our weaknesses,
but we have one who has been tempted
in every way, just as we are – yet he did not sin. Let
us then approach the throne of grace
with confidence, so that we may receive mercy
and find grace to help us in our time of need.
(Hebrews 4:15-16)

In Jesus, we have a friend and a Saviour who has been there. He knows all about our temptations, our fears, our sorrows. 'He was despised and rejected by mankind,' says the book of Isaiah. 'A man of suffering, and familiar with pain.' Even more wonderfully, he went through that suffering *for us*. That's how much he loves us! 'Surely he took up our pain and bore our suffering ... he was pierced for our transgressions, he was crushed for our iniquities; the punishment that brought us peace was on him, and by his wounds we are healed.'

The suffering servant Isaiah spoke of the Saviour who invites us to draw near to him right now, today. In whatever trials or struggles we're currently facing. As an old hymn reminds us, there is no other friend like this one:

> Can we find a Friend so faithful
> Who will all our sorrows share?
> Jesus knows our every weakness,
> Take it to the Lord in prayer.[1]

1. 'What A Friend We Have In Jesus', Joseph M. Scriven (1855) https://www.allthelyrics.com/lyrics/pink/dont_let_me_get_me-lyrics-22507.html.

To those who let him in, to those who allow him to walk alongside them through the ups and downs of life in this world, Jesus makes a wonderful promise. 'I am with you always. I will never leave you, nor forsake you.'

We don't have to be alone any more.

Holding on

But sometimes our feelings don't follow, do they? Sometimes even when we know something to be true in our heads, we don't feel it in our hearts. If we are believers in Jesus, he has promised that he is always with us. But sometimes when we're in the grip of depression, we might struggle to believe that. We feel so alone, so abandoned.

As he hung on the cross, Jesus himself used words from a Psalm to cry out to God. 'My God, my God, why have you forsaken me?' (Psalm 22:1). The Psalm goes on:

> Why are you so far from saving me,
> so far from my cries of anguish?

133

My God, I cry out by day, but you do not answer,
by night, but I find no rest
(Psalm 22:1-2).

No one has ever been as alone as Jesus was in that moment. As he took upon himself the penalty for sin, Jesus experienced a complete separation from his Father, a severing of the loving relationship they had enjoyed for all eternity. He experienced that ultimate, incomparable loneliness, so that we don't have to.

If we have put our trust in Jesus, we can trust in Jesus' promises, even when we *feel* far from him. He is the Good Shepherd who will never abandon his sheep. 'I give them eternal life, and they shall never perish,' he says. 'No one can snatch them out of my hand' (John 10:28). When we wonder if we're going to make it, we can rest in the knowledge that it is not about us holding on to Jesus, but about him holding on to us.

When I fear my faith will fail,
Christ will hold me fast;
When the tempter would prevail,
He will hold me fast.

I could never keep my hold
Through life's fearful path;
For my love is often cold;
He must hold me fast.[2]

Back there on that warm May day in my parents' garden, when I grasped to find some words that would offer comfort, I wondered why my faith in Jesus didn't seem to change anything. I couldn't seem to pray properly, or for any length of time. I couldn't really concentrate on the Bible. Sometimes friends would visit and read it to me, which helped. My own faith felt so weak and inadequate. But thankfully, God was holding on to me. Depression couldn't separate me from his love.

Walking with the Shepherd

Psalm 23 is probably the most famous of the Psalms, and for good reason. When we read it with the New Testament in mind, it takes on new meaning. Jesus is the shepherd who walks with us and guides us, through both the

---

2. 'He Will Hold Me Fast', 2013 Getty Music Publishing/Matt Merker Music (BMI).

green pastures and the dark valleys. We can trust him to take care of us, even when we can't see the way ahead, and shadows seem to loom on every side. He will bring us safely through the dark places, and one day out the other side into the light.

The LORD is my shepherd, I lack nothing.
He makes me lie down in green pastures,
he leads me beside quiet waters,
he refreshes my soul.
He guides me along the right paths
for his name's sake.
Even though I walk through the darkest valley,
I will fear no evil, for you are with me;
your rod and your staff, they comfort me.
You prepare a table before me
in the presence of my enemies.
You anoint my head with oil; my cup overflows.
Surely your goodness and love will follow me
all the days of my life,
and I will dwell in the house of the LORD forever
(Psalm 23).

Something to try...

- Read Psalm 23 aloud as a prayer.

Something to remember...

As Christians, our confidence in God doesn't rest on anything we've done, but only on what Jesus has done. Our feelings may go up and down, but God's love for us will never change.

What did Jesus say?

My sheep listen to my voice; I know them, and they follow me. I give them eternal life, and they shall never perish; no one will snatch them out of my hand (John 10:27-28).

WHAT NEXT?

I found out the hard way.

Simply being a Christian wasn't going to take away my struggles with depression. But I still felt for a long time that if I could just see things differently, just change my perspective or have enough faith, then I would finally get this 'sorted'. Things would carry on for a while, and I'd be just fine. But then, every so often, I'd find the familiar emptiness and fear beginning to return.

I remember going for an early evening walk, during one of those times of struggling. I was living close to the sea, and it was a great blessing to stroll along the seemingly endless promenade, drinking in the beauty of a red gold sunset. But my bitter thoughts were at odds with the tranquillity of the scene. I felt so frustrated and fed up. Things had been going fine for some time, and now here I was again facing the same old inner battle. What was the matter with me? Would I always be this way? Why hadn't God taken this struggle away?

But on that walk, a Bible verse came to mind that would help me begin to see things differently. It was a verse from one of the letters the apostle Paul wrote, in which he speaks of a struggle he had been having. Paul calls this struggle his 'thorn', and no one knows exactly what it was; perhaps an illness or physical affliction of some kind. Paul doesn't say, but he does tell us that he prayed for God to take it away:

Three times I pleaded with the Lord
to take it away from me.
But he said to me, 'My grace is sufficient for you,
for my power is made perfect in weakness'
(2 Corinthians 12:8-9).

God didn't take Paul's thorn away. As I walked that day, I thought a lot about this verse, and about depression – my own 'thorn'. I began to think about what life would be like if I didn't struggle with depression anymore. I might start thinking I was doing pretty well in life, I thought. I might not realise just how much I needed God. I might not find myself on my knees like I was right now, crying out to him for help. And maybe that was exactly where I needed to be.

Will it happen again?

Many people who have recovered from an episode of severe depression live in fear of relapse, as I did. They worry about when, and if, their depression will return.

If you have been through a period of severe depression and come out the other side, it is natural that you might worry about whether it will happen again. No one can really answer that question, because everyone is different. Some people might only ever suffer one major depressive episode, especially if their depression was triggered by a specific life event. Others might find, like me, that their depression does return.

Depression is not an easy thing to struggle with. No one would choose it. When I realised that it wasn't ever going to disappear from my life completely, I did sometimes feel quite frustrated and sorry for myself.

But as time went on, I began to meet more and more people who struggled with depression themselves. And other things too. Anxiety. Loneliness. Grief. Chronic health conditions. Insecurity. Disappointment. Hope-lessness.

We don't have to live too long in this world to realise that life isn't easy for anybody.

The big difference for the Christian is the promise we have in Jesus:

I will be with you always.
I will never leave you, nor forsake you.
(Matthew 28:20, Hebrews 13:5)

And if you are a Christian, one of the ways God will keep that promise is through *you.* There is a wonderful verse in the Bible that describes how this works:

Praise be to the God and Father
of our Lord Jesus Christ, the Father of compassion
and the God of all comfort,
who comforts us in all our troubles,
so that we can comfort those in any trouble
with the comfort we ourselves receive from God
(2 Corinthians 1:3-4).

When you have been through difficult times yourself, you are in a much better position to help other people. You know what it's like to struggle. You probably have a lot more compassion towards other people who are struggling, and a lot more understanding of how they might feel. This is a precious, precious gift! I can promise you that if you are willing, you will have many opportunities ahead to offer this kind of comfort to other people, people you may not even know yet.

One word of caution though. As this book has emphasised, depression can be a very different experience for different people. So be careful not to assume you know how someone else is feeling, or what they are going through. I'm sorry to say that I have sometimes made that mistake with people. One of the best things we can do is really listen to others, and pray for them. That doesn't mean we shouldn't share our own experiences, or offer advice. Sometimes that will be really helpful, but we have to do it with humility, recognising that we don't have all the answers!

Life after depression

Depression is rarely a constant, unchanging thing. Most people who go through a period of severe depression will get better. Even those who have struggled with depression many times may find that their depressive episodes get milder, or last for a shorter time. Depression sufferers often learn what helps them the most, and develop a 'toolbox' of strategies to help them cope with low moods. They learn to spot the warning signs that show they are beginning to struggle, and to seek help before things get worse.

This has certainly been the case in my own life. I have continued to struggle with depression off and on, but it hasn't stayed the same. By God's grace, it has never been as severe as it was during my teenage years. There are patterns to it; for instance, I know I'm more likely to get depressed when I'm over-busy and stressed, or if something really sad happens. I'm still learning, but as time goes on I've come to understand more about depression and more about myself. Most importantly, I've come to understand more about God.

Sometimes I can even thank him for my struggles with depression. Without them, I might think that I could manage life perfectly well by myself. I might fail to see how much I need him, and I might forget to cry out to Him for the help that, truthfully, we *all* need.

I don't know what the future has in store for you, but I do know that however long you struggle with depression for in this lifetime, it won't last forever. In Heaven, where the Christian believer will spend eternity with God, *there will be no depression.* 'He will wipe every tear from their eyes,' says the book of Revelation. 'There will be no more death or mourning or crying or pain, for the old order of things has passed away' (Revelation 21:4). We can look forward to a future where all our mental health struggles will be forgotten, where we will know complete and perfect health in body and mind.

> For our light and momentary troubles
> are achieving for us an eternal glory that far
> outweighs them all.
> So we fix our eyes not on what is seen,
> but on what is unseen, since what is seen is
> temporary, but what is unseen is eternal
> (2 Corinthians 4:17-18).

From wailing to dancing

> I will exalt you, LORD,
> for you lifted me out of the depths
> and did not let my enemies gloat over me.
> LORD my God, I called to you for help,
> and you healed me.
> You, LORD, brought me up from

the realm of the dead;
you spared me from going down to the pit.

Sing the praises of the LORD,
you his faithful people;
praise his holy name.
For his anger lasts only a moment,
but his favour lasts a lifetime;
weeping may stay for the night,
but rejoicing comes in the morning.
When I felt secure, I said,
'I shall never be shaken.'
LORD, when you favoured me,
you made my royal mountain stand firm;
but when you hid your face,
I was dismayed.

To you, LORD, I called;
to the LORD I cried for mercy:
'What is gained if I am silenced,
if I go down to the pit?
Will the dust praise you?
Will it proclaim your faithfulness?
Hear, LORD, and be merciful to me;
LORD, be my help.'

You turned my wailing into dancing;
you removed my sackcloth
and clothed me with joy,
that my heart may sing your praises
and not be silent.
LORD my God, I will praise you for ever
(Psalm 30).

It's been really difficult choosing which Psalms to include in this book. So many of them speak into our most painful times with eloquence and insight. That's why I'd encourage you to delve into the Psalms yourself, and find your own favourites. Find those which speak most powerfully to you, Psalms you can pray and make your own.

Psalm 30 is a great one to end with because it captures both the highs and lows of life in this fallen world.

'Weeping may stay for the night, but rejoicing comes in the morning,' the psalmist proclaims. This has been my experience, and the experience of many who have walked through seasons of pain and sorrow.

There really is hope for those of us who suffer with depression. Our greatest hope, our ultimate hope, is found in the God of the Bible. The psalmist is absolutely clear who it is that has brought about this turnaround in his circumstances – **the Lord** is the one who has lifted him out of the depths, brought him up from the realm of the dead, spared him from going down to the pit.

'YOU turned my wailing into dancing,' he declares. 'YOU removed my sackcloth and clothed me with joy.'

My prayer for you is that you would turn to God in your depression. He has promised never to turn away *anyone* who comes to him. He has promised his constant presence, his loving care and his transforming grace to all who recognise their need and come to him. Because the truth is that we are all needy people. We all desperately need the forgiveness and healing only Jesus can give.

The psalmist testifies to the miracles that God can work in the darkest of times. Believers through the ages can echo his words, for they have lived this story.

Weeping may remain for the night, but there will be rejoicing. There will be dancing.

LORD my God, I will praise you forever. Amen.

Something to try...

- Look back through this book and remind yourself of the things you've found most helpful.

Something to remember...

Your struggle with depression won't last forever. But while it does last, God has promised his constant presence, his loving care and his transforming grace to all who come to him through faith in Jesus.

What did Jesus say?

My grace is sufficient for you, for my power is made perfect in weakness (2 Corinthians 12:9).

PLACES TO TURN FOR HELP (UK)

If you are struggling with depression, please talk to someone. The best person to start with would be a parent or other trusted adult, such as a teacher or church leader. Please also think seriously about making an appointment with your doctor. They will be very used to seeing people who are battling with symptoms of depression.

If you need someone to talk to right now, anonymously, please consider calling one of the helplines below. The websites listed also contain lots of support and information for those struggling with their mental health.

U.K.
Samaritans
If you are in distress and need someone to talk to, you can ring Samaritans free any day time day or night on 116 123. www.samaritans.org.uk

YoungMinds Crisis Messenger
Provides free, 24/7 crisis support across the UK. If you are experiencing a mental health crisis, just text YM to 85258. www.youngminds.org.uk

Childline
If you are under 19, you can call, email or chat online about any problem, large or small.
Freephone 24/7: 0800 1111; www.childline.org.uk

Biblical Counselling UK
www.biblicalcounselling.org.uk
E-mail: info@biblicalcounselling.org.uk

U.S.A.
CCEF
https://www.ccef.org/counselor-information-request-form/

Association of Biblical Counselors
https://christiancounseling.com/network/find-a-counselor/

AUSTRALIA
The Resilience Centre
https://www.theresiliencecentre.com.au/ – Lyn Worsley is the founder (a committed Christian) and or Colleen Hirst & Associates http://merrylandscounselling.com.au/doctor/colleen-hirst/

RECOMMENDED READING

About the Christian Faith

Changing Lanes by Jonny Pearse (10 Publishing, 2013)

A Sneaking Suspicion by John Dickson (Matthias Media, 1992)

The Case for Christ for Kids by Lee Strobel (Zonderkidz, 2010)

The Case for Christ, Student Edition by Lee Strobel (Zondervan, 2014)

Turning Points by Vaughan Roberts (Authentic Media, 1999)

About Mental Health

Dealing with Depression by Sarah Collins and Jayne Haynes (Christian Focus, 2015)

Eating Disorders by Emma Scrivener (Day One, 2016)

A New Name by Emma Scrivener (IVP, September 2012)

A Student's Guide to Anxiety by Edward T. Welch (Christian Focus, March 2020)

Life Hacks
Letting God Sort It
by Mary-Louise Stone

Choices and challenges – that's life. But how do we face up to them? Developing strategies and techniques to make our existence easy might seem like a good idea – and, let's face it, there are plenty of distractions around! But surely there's more to life than smartphones and endless playlists? Let God manage your life through his Word. Here are fifty to the point devotionals that will focus your mind on God and his 'hacks' for living the life he created us to live.

ISBN: 978-1-5271-0046-6

TRAIL BLAZERS

• Charles Spurgeon •

THE PRINCE OF PREACHERS

Christian Timothy George

Charles Spurgeon
Prince of Preachers
by Christian George

Charles Spurgeon was a simple country lad who went on to become one of the best known preachers in London, Europe and the world. Caught in a snowstorm one day when he was a teenager, he crept into the back of a church and the words "Look unto Jesus and be saved!" changed his whole life. Charles spoke words that touched the hearts of rich and poor alike. His fame became so widespread that it is reputed that even Queen Victoria went to hear one of his sermons. Charles was more concerned about the King of Kings – Jesus Christ.

ISBN: 978-1-78191-528-8

• Martyn Lloyd-Jones •

FROM WALES TO WESTMINSTER

Christopher Catherwood